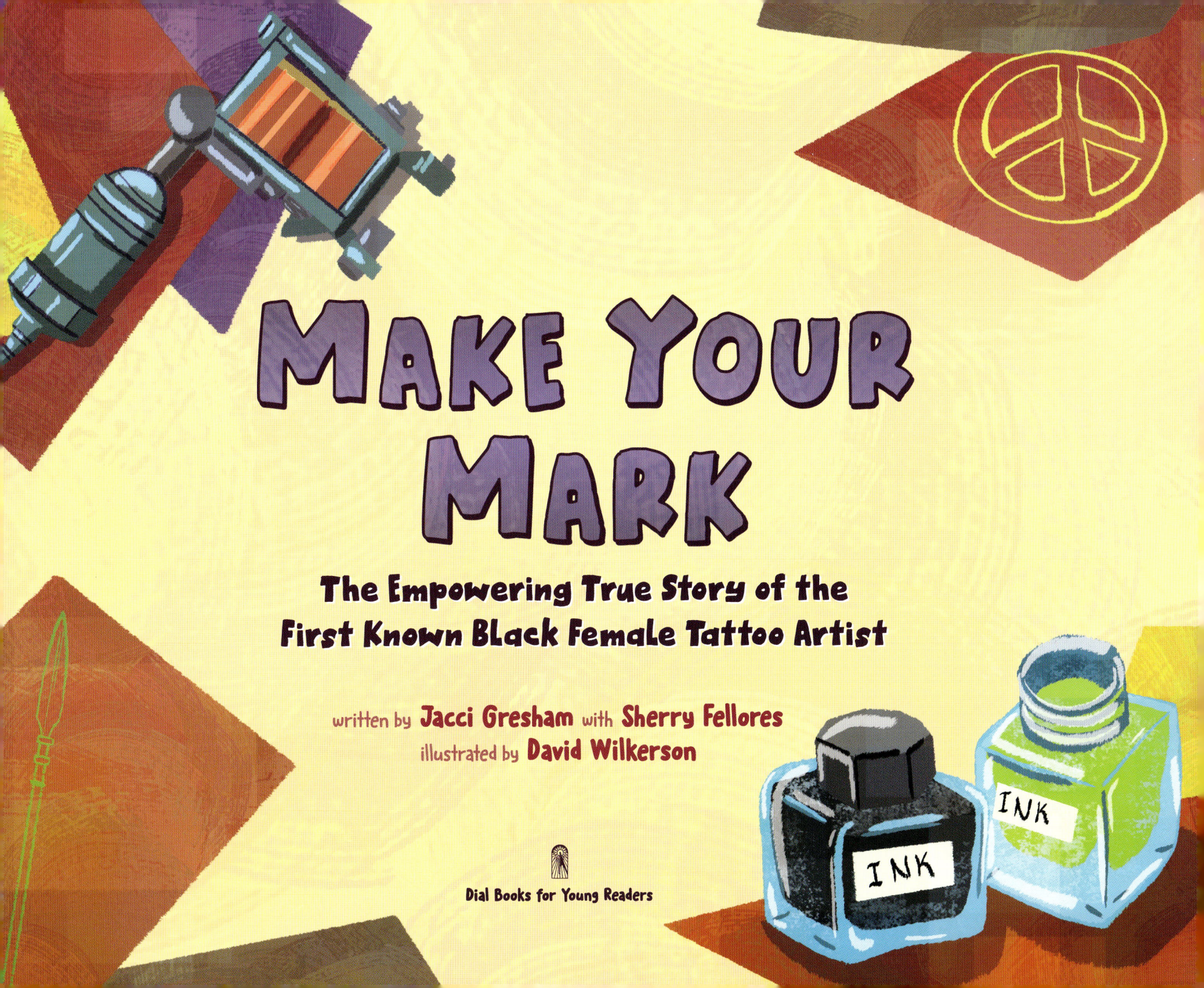

MAKE YOUR MARK

The Empowering True Story of the First Known Black Female Tattoo Artist

written by **Jacci Gresham** with **Sherry Fellores**
illustrated by **David Wilkerson**

Dial Books for Young Readers

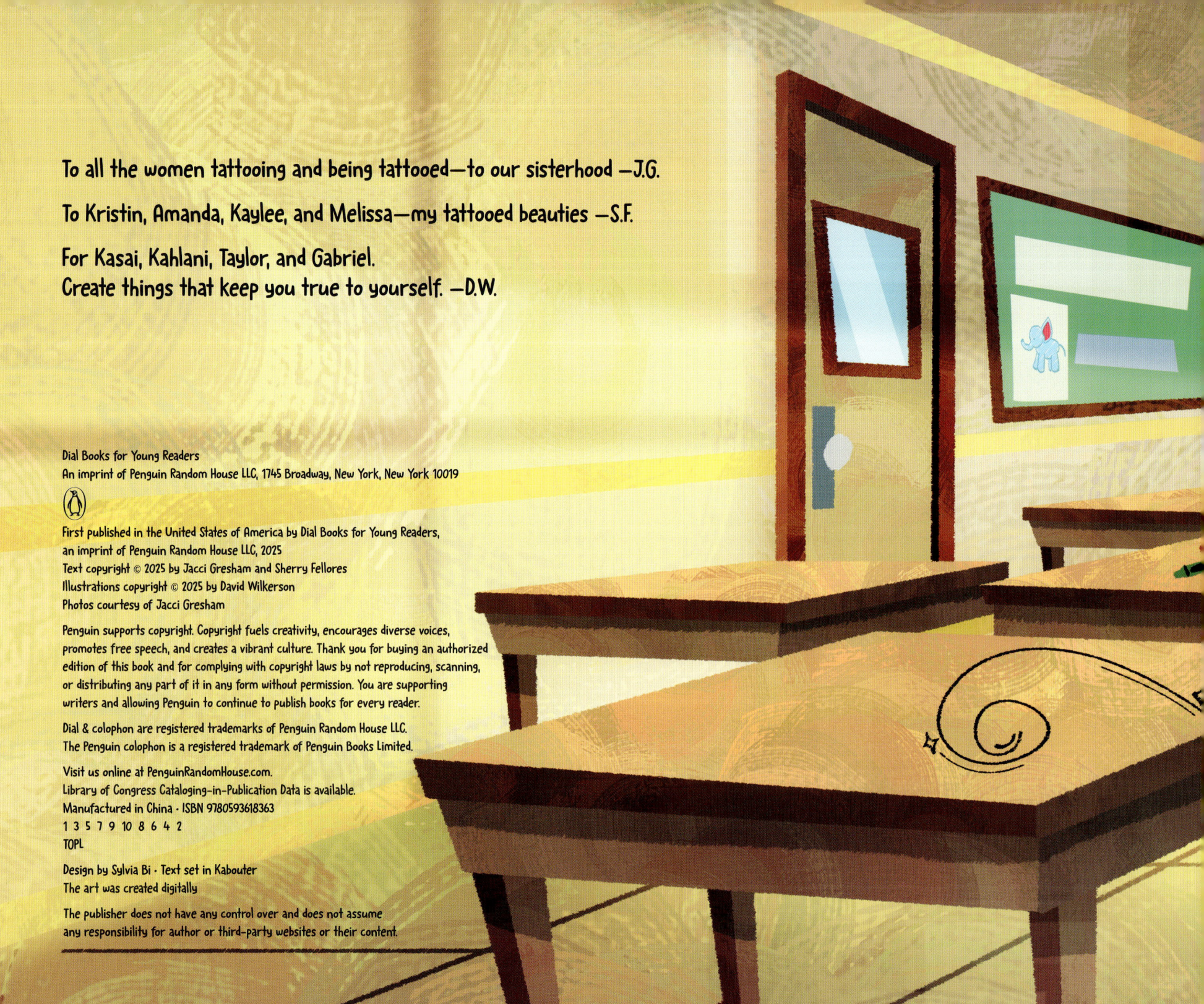

To all the women tattooing and being tattooed—to our sisterhood —J.G.

To Kristin, Amanda, Kaylee, and Melissa—my tattooed beauties —S.F.

For Kasai, Kahlani, Taylor, and Gabriel.
Create things that keep you true to yourself. —D.W.

Dial Books for Young Readers
An imprint of Penguin Random House LLC, 1745 Broadway, New York, New York 10019

First published in the United States of America by Dial Books for Young Readers,
an imprint of Penguin Random House LLC, 2025
Text copyright © 2025 by Jacci Gresham and Sherry Fellores
Illustrations copyright © 2025 by David Wilkerson
Photos courtesy of Jacci Gresham

Dial & colophon are registered trademarks of Penguin Random House LLC.
The Penguin colophon is a registered trademark of Penguin Books Limited.

Visit us online at PenguinRandomHouse.com.
Library of Congress Cataloging-in-Publication Data is available.
Manufactured in China · ISBN 9780593618363
1 3 5 7 9 10 8 6 4 2
TOPL

Design by Sylvia Bi · Text set in Kabouter
The art was created digitally

FIRST, STRAY OUTSIDE THE LINES

I step into the art classroom for the first time. The smell of paint stirs my soul.
I pour my feelings onto paper like liquid—a sweep of the brush here, a dab of color there.

"Stay in the lines," says my teacher.
But for me, straying outside is more fun.

EXPRESS YOURSELF

My family doesn't have a lot of money—not even a car. But we always find ways to express ourselves. Mama sews my clothes by hand, and I strut down the hallway like a runway model. Soon, I thread and stitch short skirts, plumed hats, and more.

My own designs come to life. My body is the canvas for my unique style!

One day, I strut right into the living room
and my eyes land on the television.
"What are they doing, Daddy?"

"Making their voices heard, baby.
Fighting for equal rights."

I pick up my black marker and
draw a peace sign on my arm.

FOLLOW YOUR HEART

In middle school, most of the girls choose home economics to learn to cook and sew. But I choose a drafting class, where I learn to draw plans for new products and buildings. When I walk in on the first day, I take my seat.

I'm the only girl in the class, but it doesn't bother me. I belong here as much as anyone else.

In high school, I draw shapes and patterns that I learn in my art class at the Flint Institute of Arts. I love making art all day! I even think about studying art in college.

My mom convinces me to study architecture and engineering instead, though, so I can get a good paying job.

I scatter blank pages on my kitchen table and draw tall buildings. Then I start work at General Motors in Detroit, Michigan.

It sounds like fun, but as I sit at my desk, drawing straight lines day after day, my heart longs to create something curvy, squiggly, and totally my style.

So when the company loses money, and several of us lose our jobs, my heart is ready for the change.

KEEP AN OPEN MIND

I pack my bags and move to New Orleans to find work in the warm, friendly city. My friend Ali from Detroit comes too.

After we're settled, he picks up a piece of worn-down chalk. His arm strokes this way and that. He draws a big, bold eagle—a symbol of pride and freedom.

"How did you learn to do that?" I ask.

"I studied art in college. Then I learned to tattoo in England."

My mind races. An idea takes flight.

PRACTICE EVERY DAY

I decide I will become a tattoo artist, but I have no tattoo experience. I don't know any other Black tattoo artists. But I learn everything I can about the art of tattooing.

One day, a man with dark skin shows me his tattoos. I can tell the older ones have lost their quality. I see the problem. His artist didn't understand darker skin tones.

For brown skin, tattoos often look better when they are bigger and have less detail. Light colors instead of dark ones will make the tattoo stand out and keep it looking good over the years.

I look at my skin, and another idea sparks. I draw tattoo sketches, called flash, on brown paper. Until now, flash has always been drawn on white paper.

Over and over, I trace an African hunting
spear on crisp, brown paper until it's perfect.
I am proud of this work, and proud to see
African culture in my designs. I practice
with new, vibrant colors that I haven't
seen any other artists use.

I will make sure Black people see what my designs
will look like on their beautiful, brown skin.
Excitement bubbles with each new drawing and discovery.

DO WHAT SCARES YOU

Ali and I open a shop together. We call it AART Accent.
I add the extra *A* so we will be top in the phone book.

For the first year, Ali draws the outline on our customers,
then I do the coloring, so I get familiar with the tattoo machine.

When my first customer walks in, my heart pounds. Ali isn't
there. It's the first time I'm giving a tattoo entirely by myself.
I take deep breaths and steady my shaky hands.
I close my eyes. Skin is now my canvas.

A dazzling design flows from my heart through the machine in my hand.

My customer and I talk about how women are expected to hide their tattoos. How we should have the freedom to express ourselves. We know we are on the verge of a new revolution.

STAND UP FOR WHAT YOU BELIEVE

When I tell Ali about my first customer, he says tattooing women is distasteful and won't allow it in our shop. It's our first real argument.

I don't back down. Women deserve the right to tattoo art on their bodies just like men. I decide to get my own first tattoo.

I slide down into the chair. The smell of ink and metal fills the air. The butterflies in my stomach flutter. When I see my design take shape under my skin, it makes me proud.

It's now part of my story, and my skin is the storybook.

Other women begin marching into our shop, demanding the right to adorn their bodies with peace signs, butterflies, flowers, or whatever they choose.

AART ACCENT

I tattoo them all. Ali will just have to get used to it.

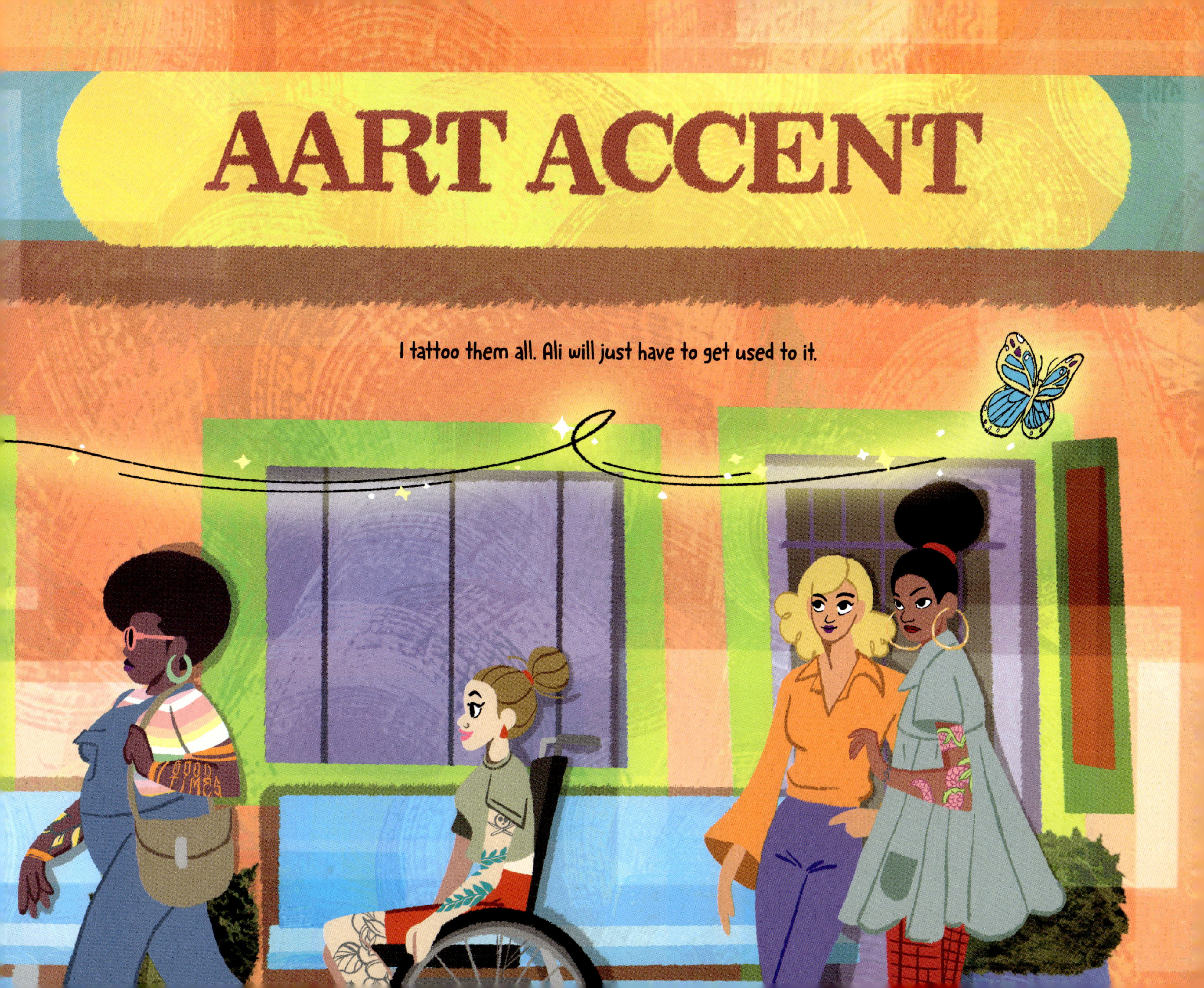

NOT EVERYONE WILL LIKE YOU—BUT LOVE YOURSELF

One day, a man who belongs to a very hateful group walks into my shop.
He scoffs at the color of my skin and scowls at me. I wonder what he's even doing here.

I smooth my shirt and stand tall.
"Here are some samples of my designs," I say.

"They are exquisite," he reluctantly admits.

Another time, a woman grows impatient as she waits her turn in my busy shop. I walk by her and she calls me a very ugly word.

"I own this shop, and I won't let you speak to me that way," I say, and I escort her out the door.

I work twice as hard to earn the respect that I deserve.

In time, the shop becomes mine alone. My mind takes me back to the peace sign I drew on my arm as a girl. I don't hold signs, march in groups, or use a big voice. I use my art and the work of my life to spread peace.

LET YOUR LIGHT SHINE

My community has a vibrancy, rhythm, and style like no other. People dance on the streets when music plays. Neighborhood pride shows on every corner.

I always jazz up our place to make it welcoming for my customers. I provide benches, plant flowers, paint the windows, and decorate for each season and holiday.

YAKAMEIN

FOOD DRIVE

DONATIONS WELCOME

Lots of people are down on their luck in my neighborhood.
Sometimes they come in because they are hungry or need extra care.
I don't turn anyone away. There is always a way to try to help.

AART ACCENT

THERE WILL BE STORMS, BUT NEVER GIVE UP!

In August 2005, Hurricane Katrina crashes into New Orleans.
The furious wind and water destroy almost everything in its path.

Thankfully, my main tattoo shop is spared. As the city rebuilds, people wander back into the shop.

I glue myself to my work area and sketch images with meaning.
I offer tattoos and symbols that represent pride in the city we love.
We share our stories and cope together.

MAKE YOUR MARK

Each time I step out of my storefront, I watch the people go by. I talk with many. Hundreds have sat in my tattoo chair, each with their unique, beautiful skin. My designs will always be a part of them, and every one of them will forever be a part of me.

AUTHOR'S NOTE:

When I open the scrapbook to my mind, I think of all the places I've been. So many fluttery flights to unknown destinations—as if a curious butterfly somewhere deep in my soul led the way. Following that butterfly helped me find my way back to the hand-drawn art I loved so well as a kid. I didn't set out to be a trailblazer, but that's what happened. Along the way, I made history by becoming America's very first female African American tattoo artist, doing what I love while making my mark.

—Jacci Gresham